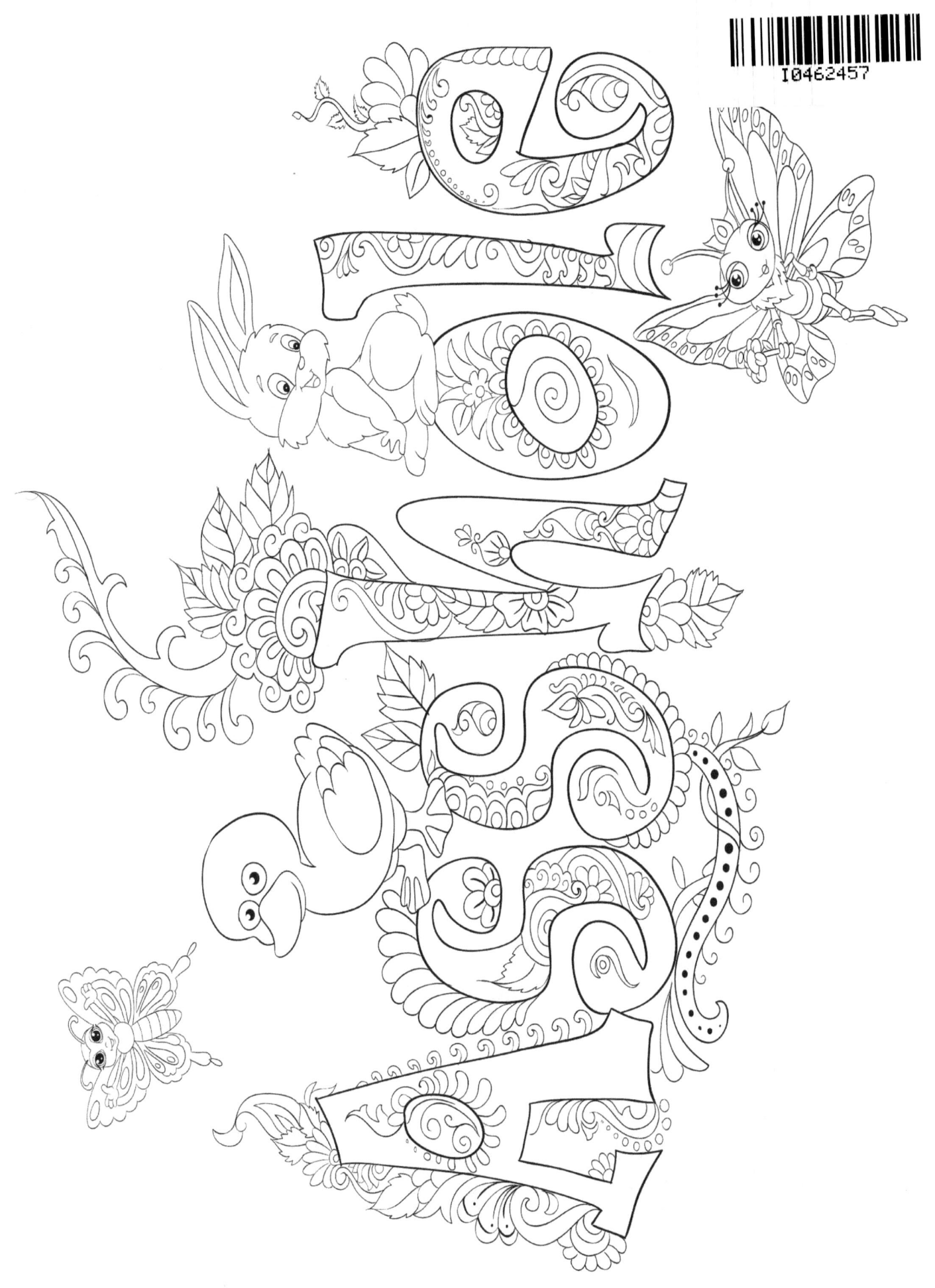

ISBN: 978-1523868094

Illustrated by:
    Mandala & Caricature Illustration
    Joshua Lazana Lagman and Jade Villaremo

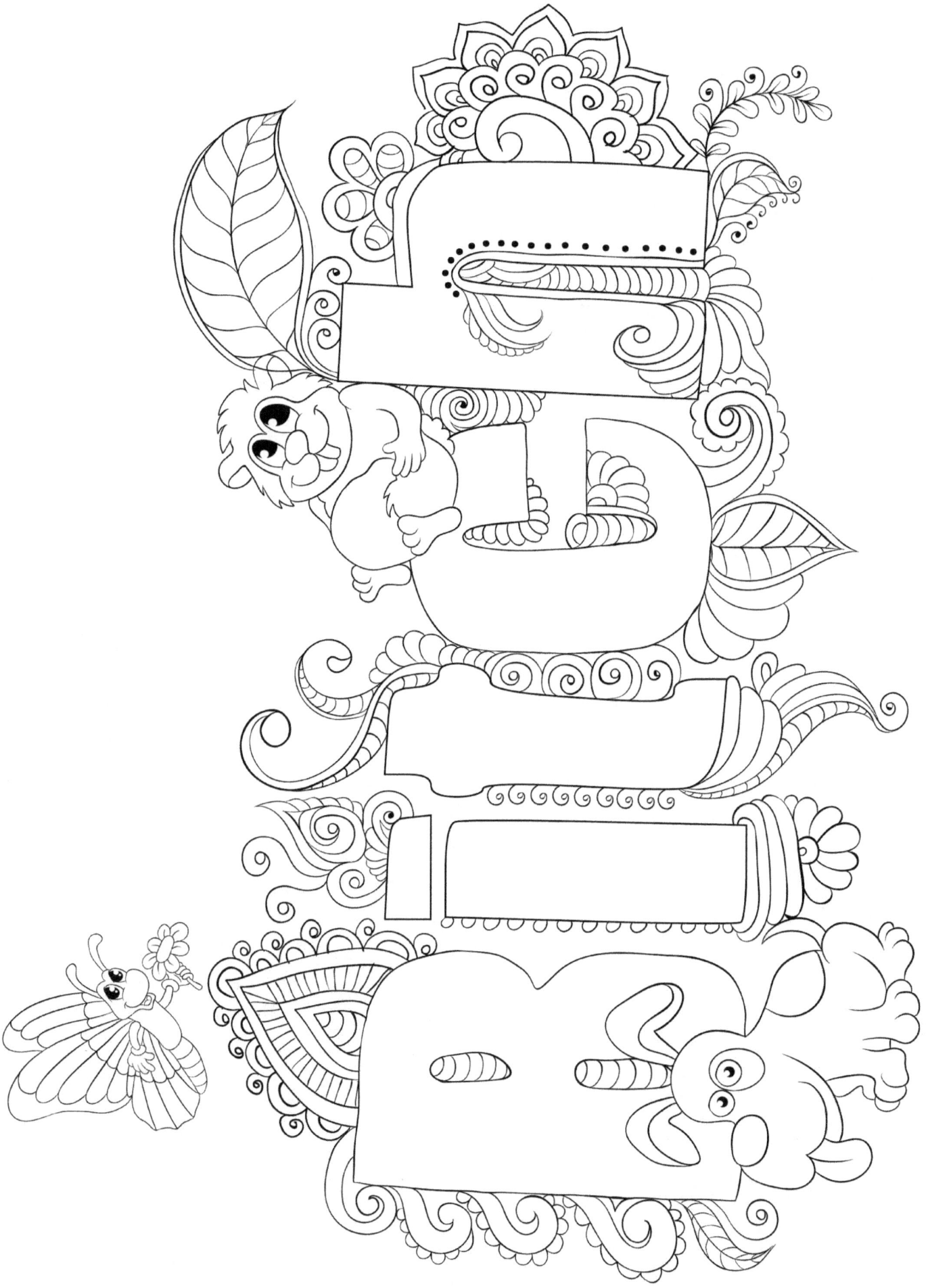

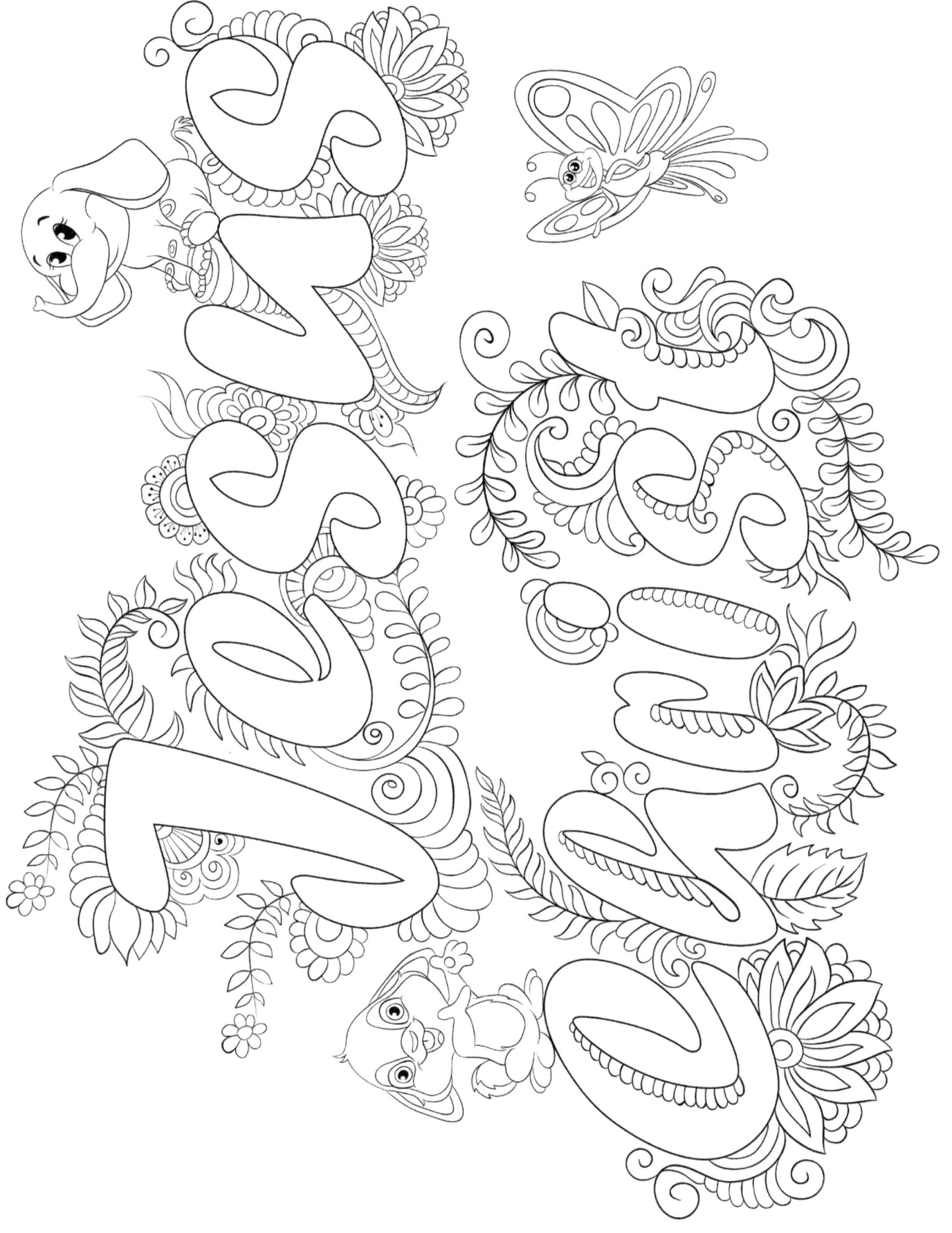

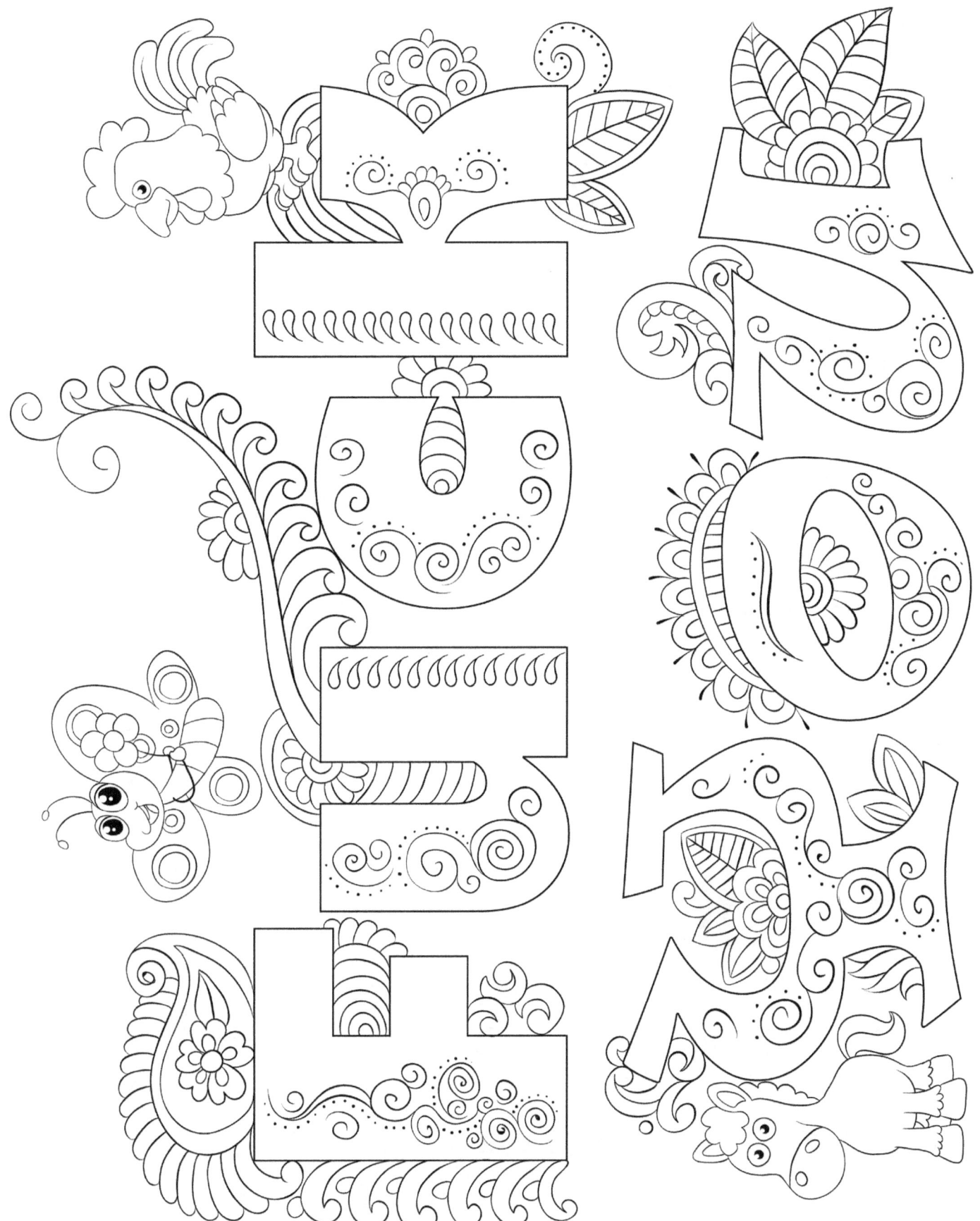

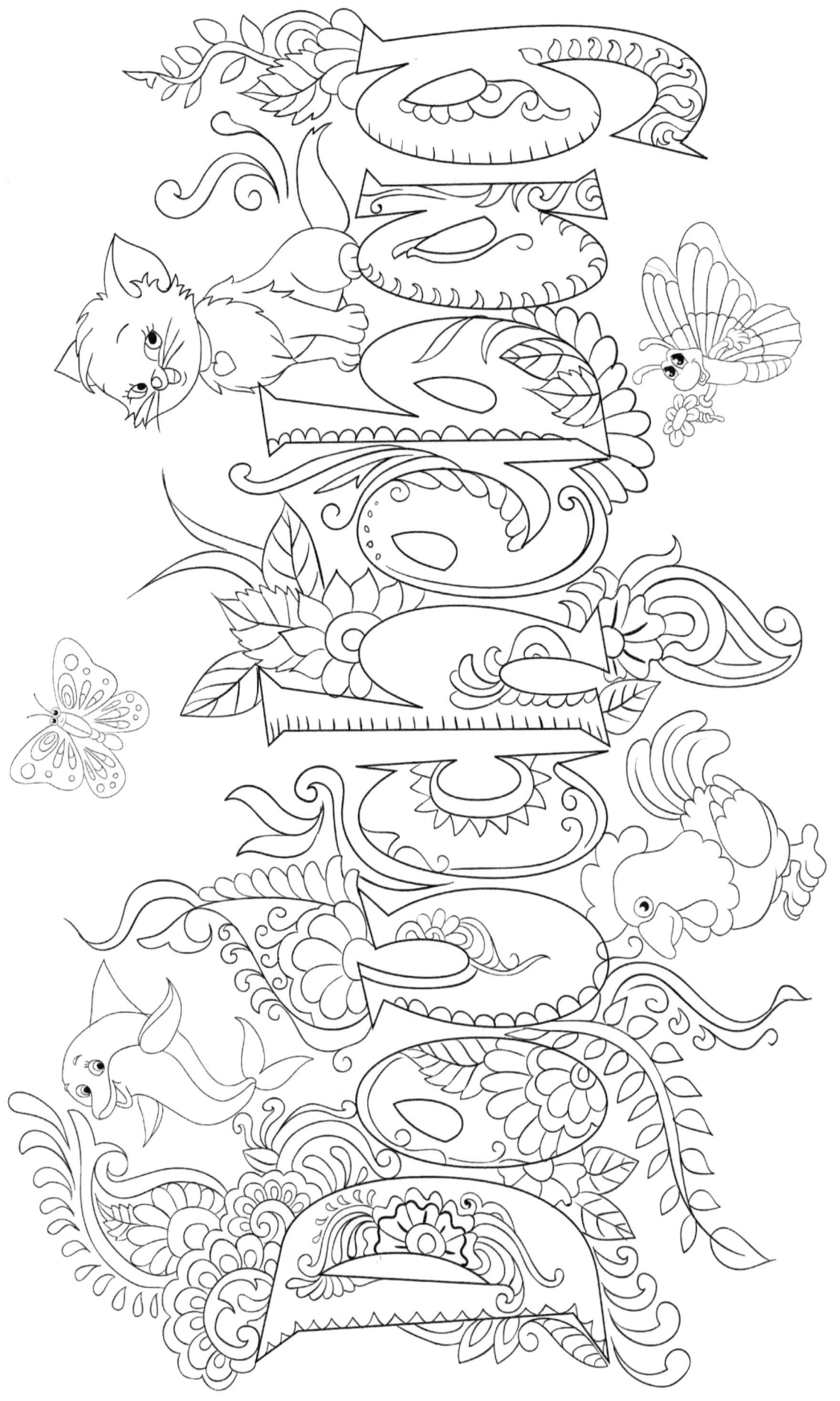

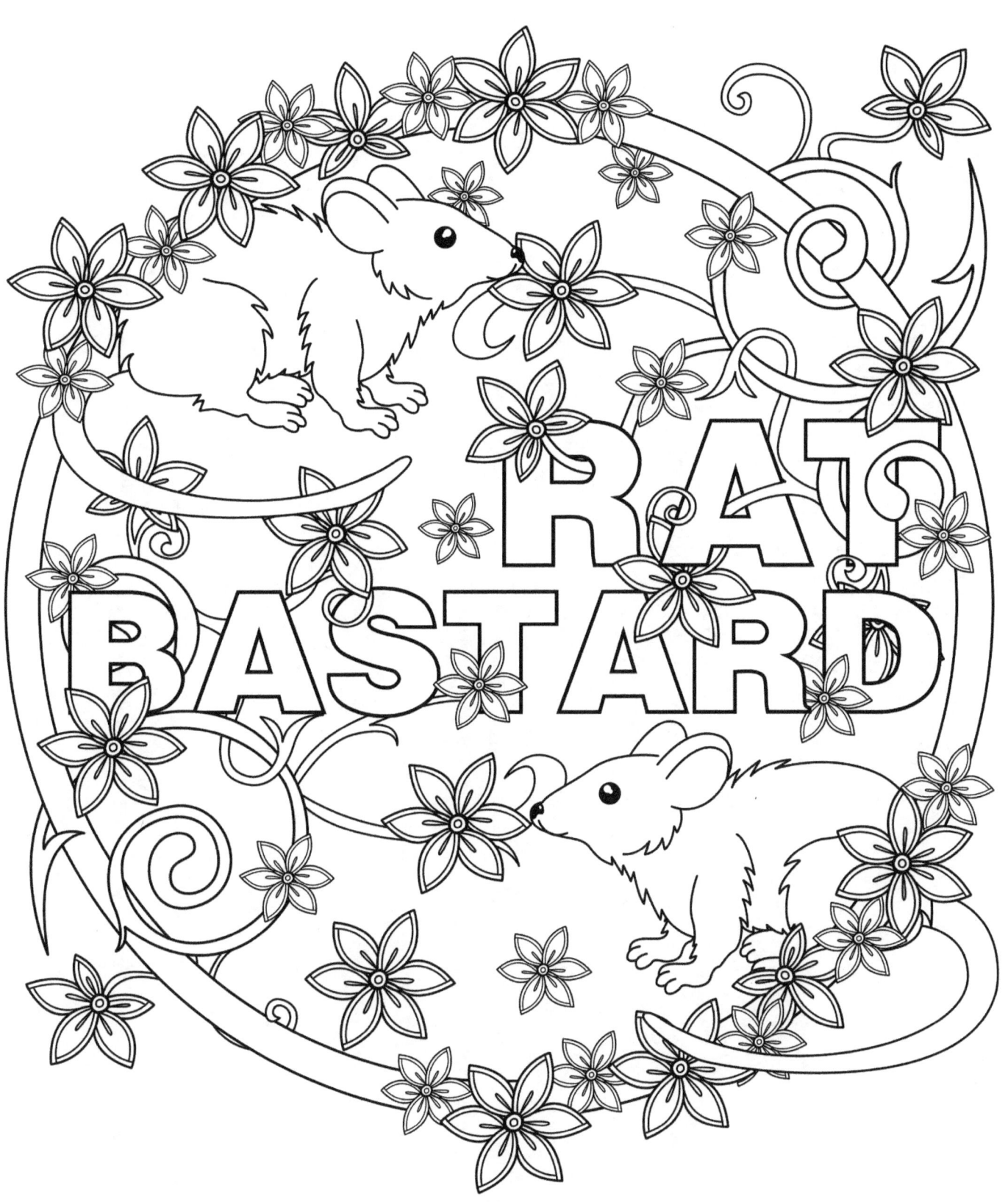

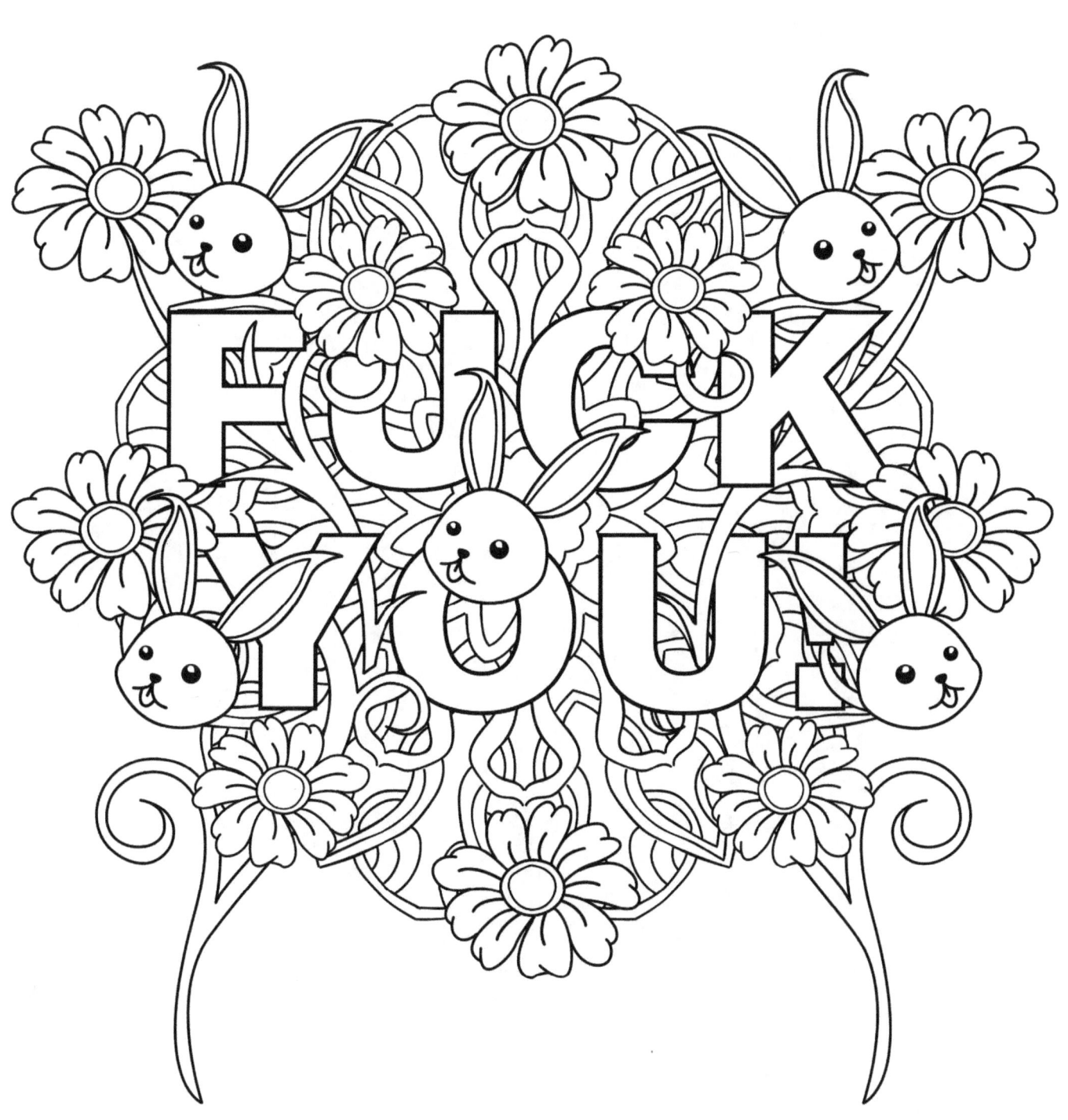

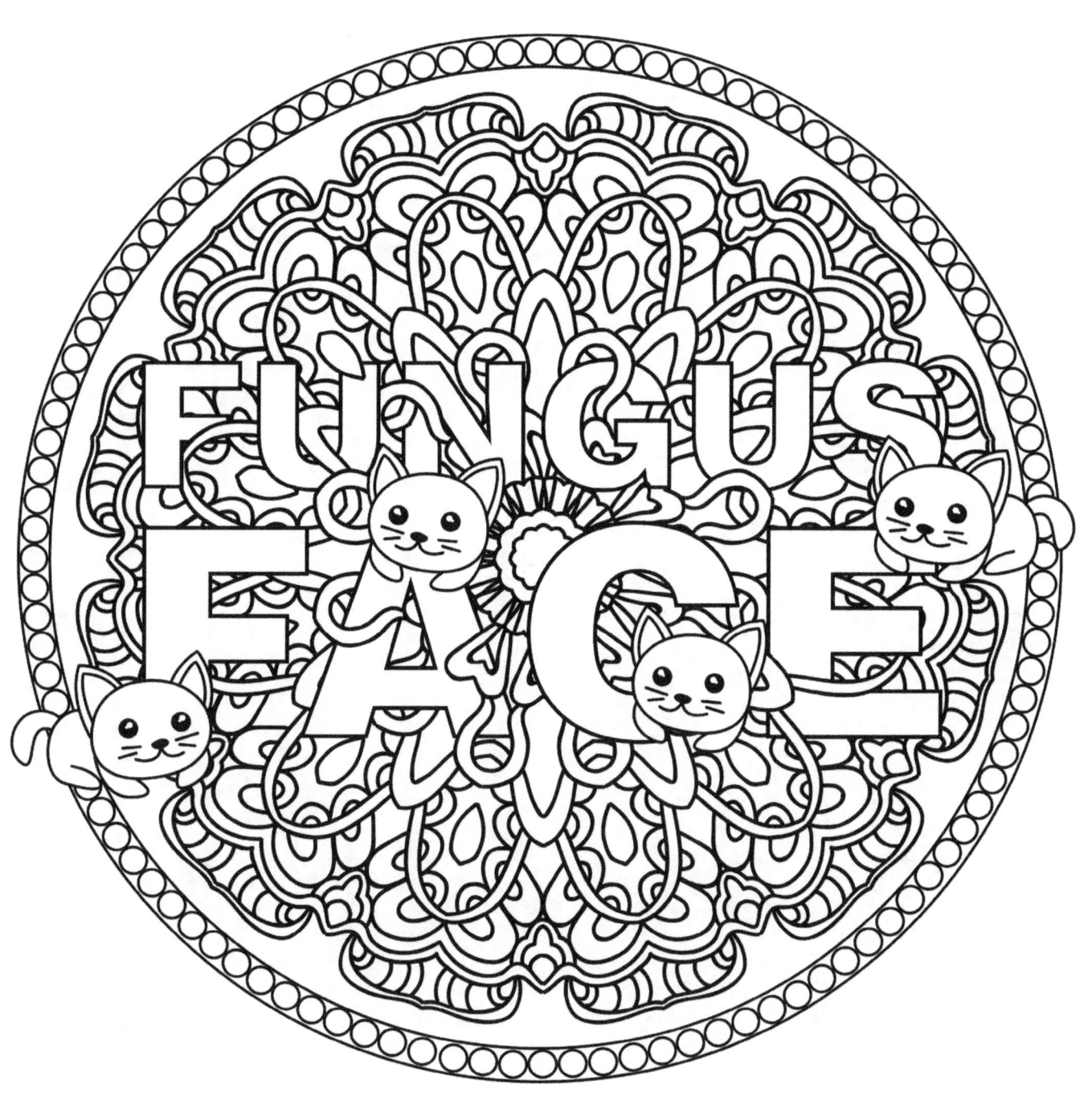

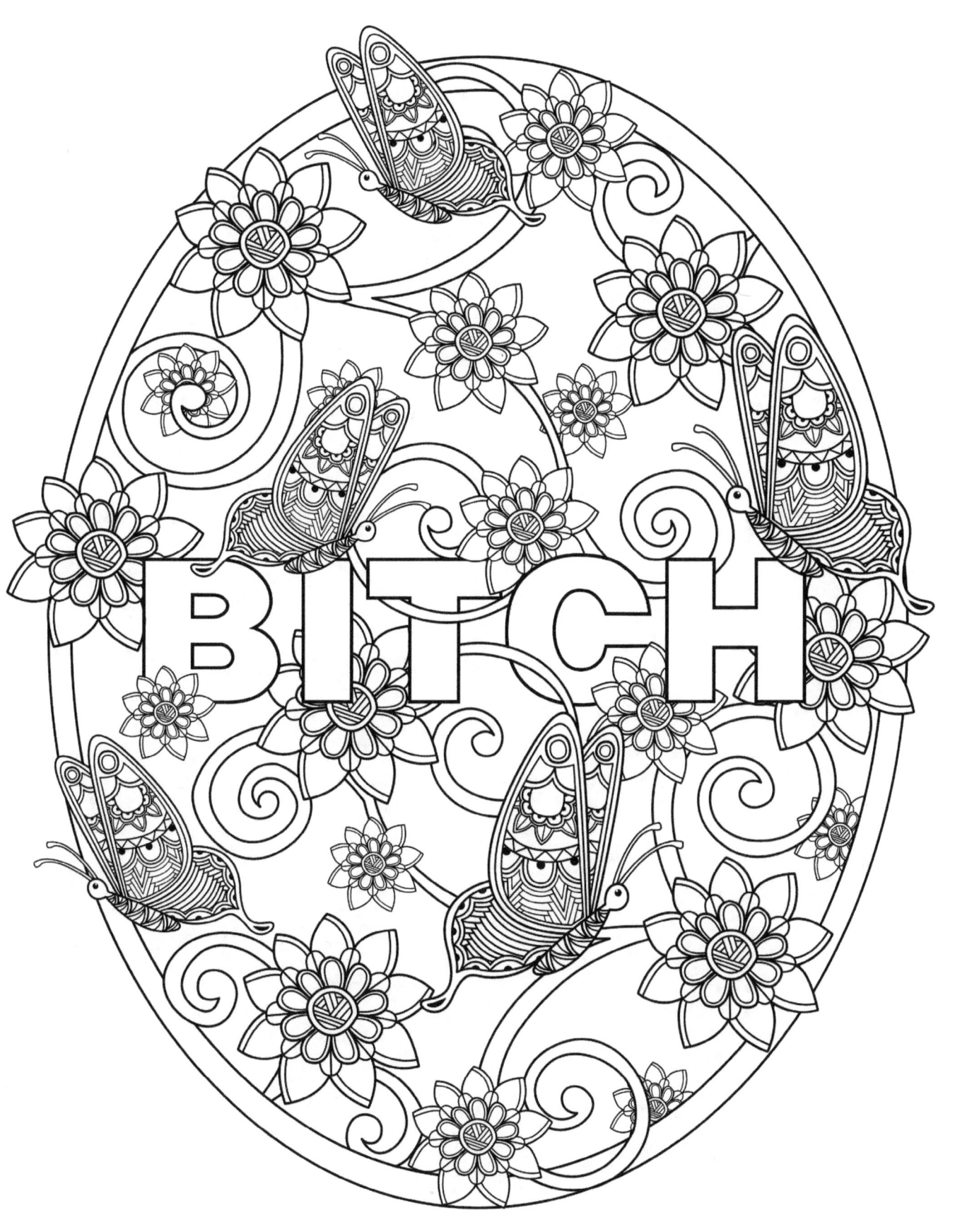

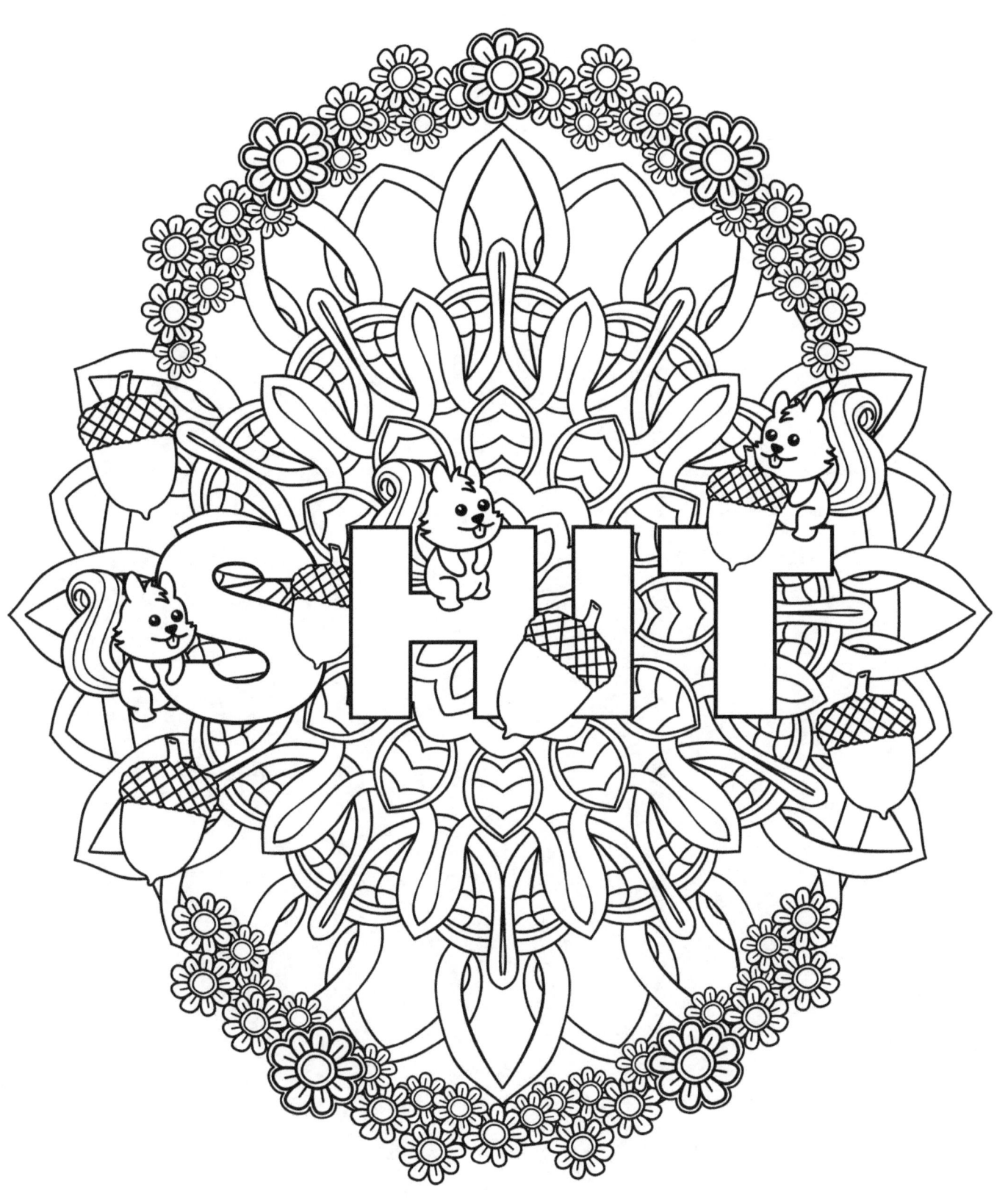

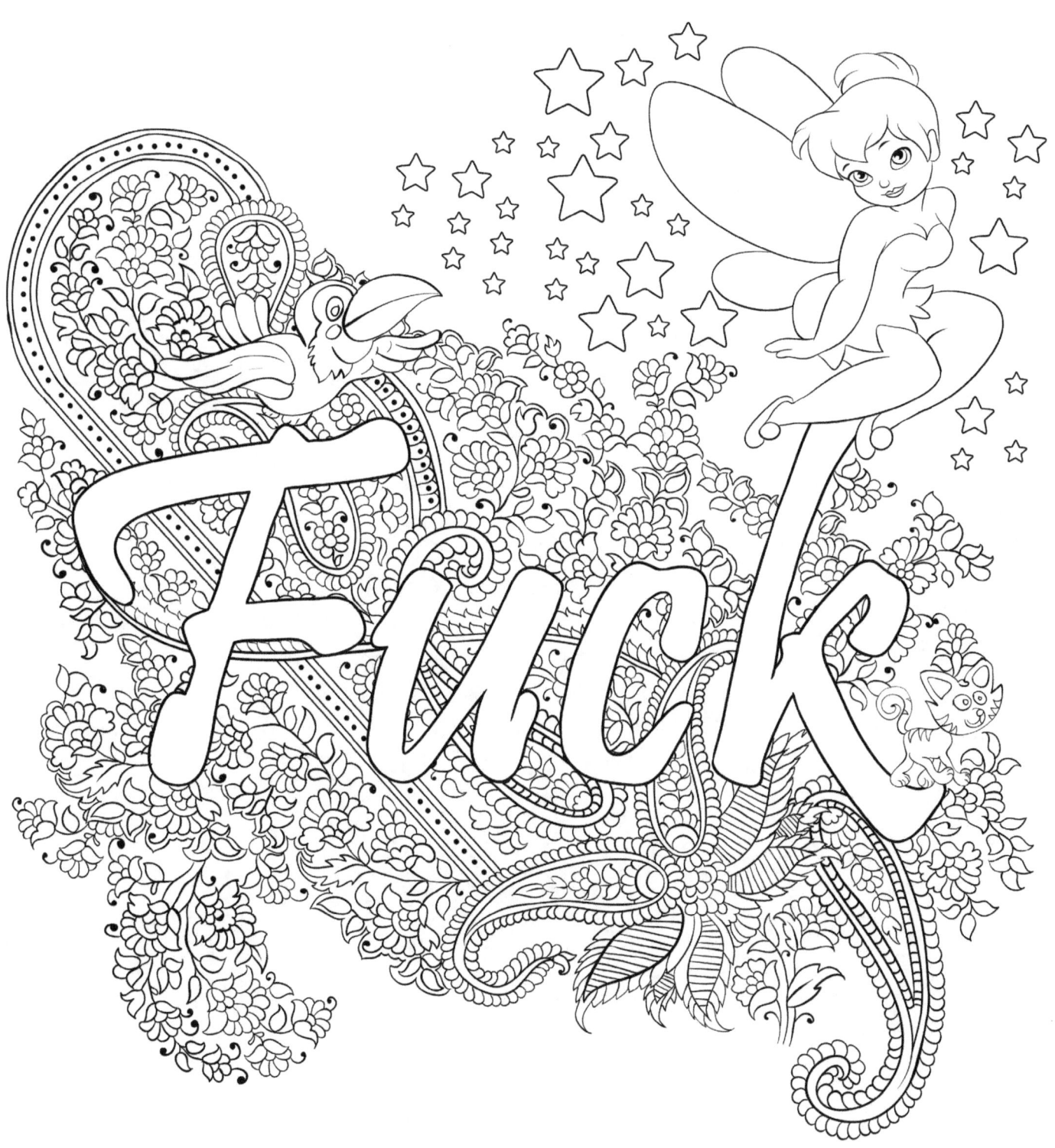

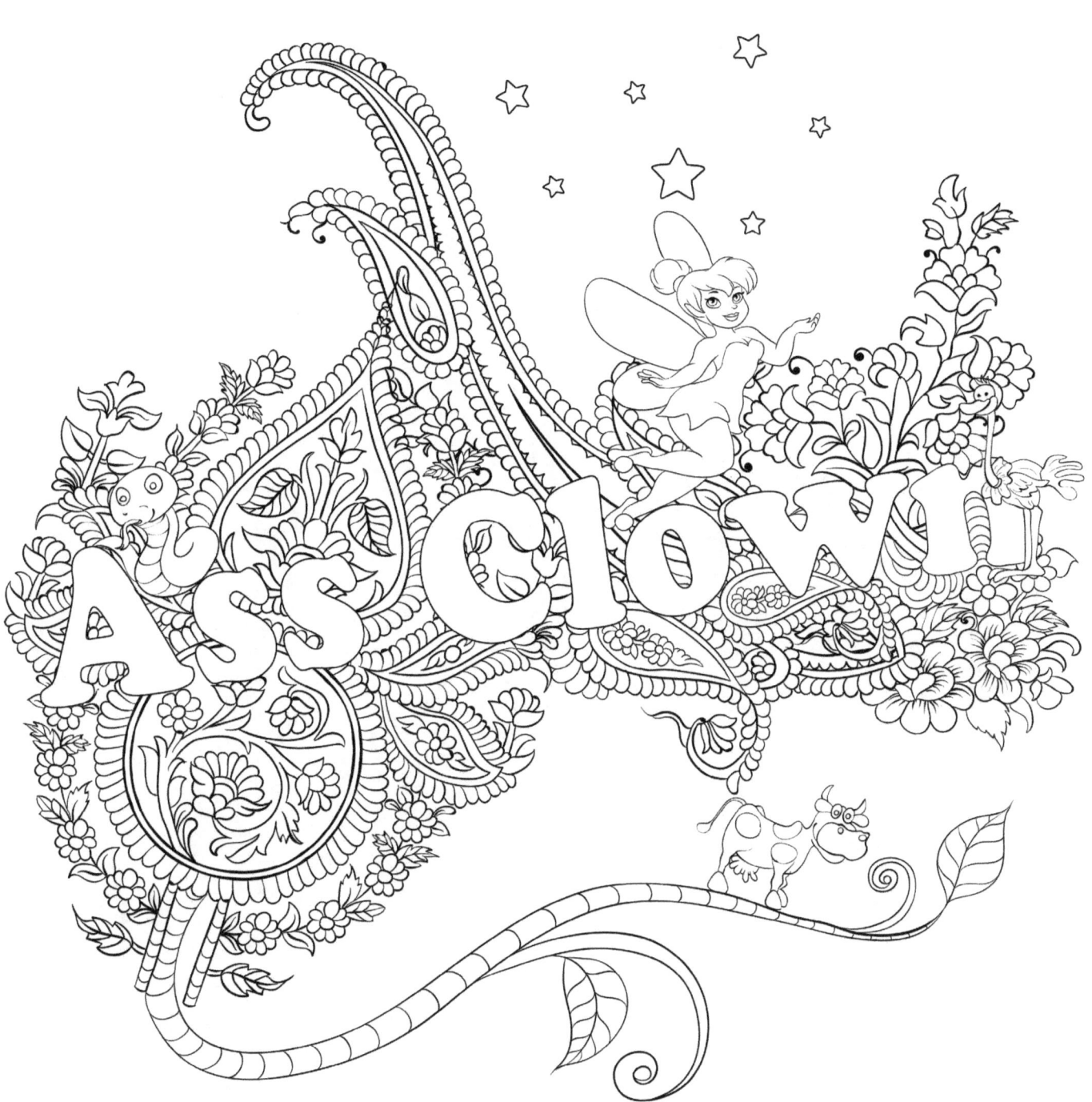

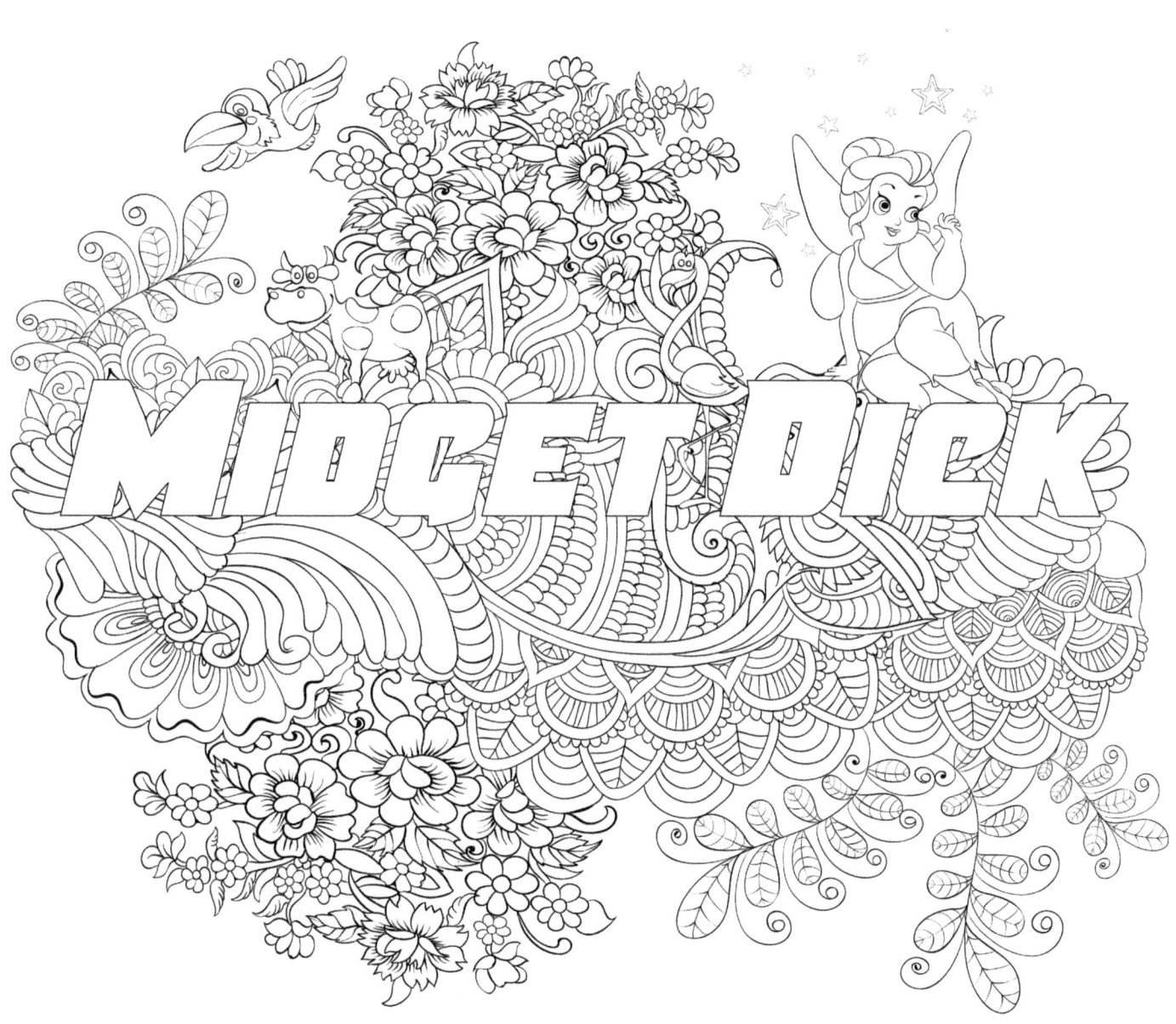

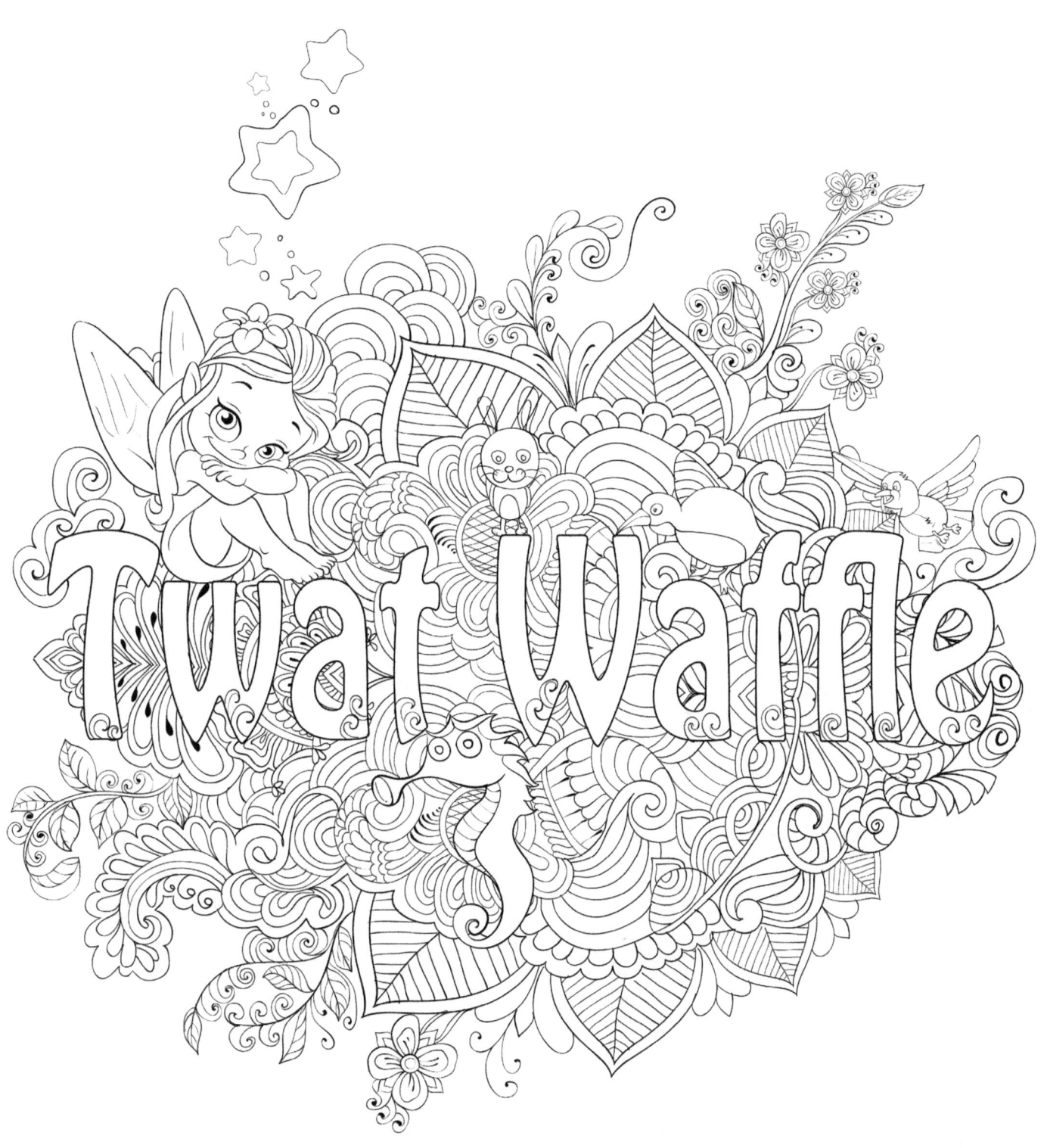

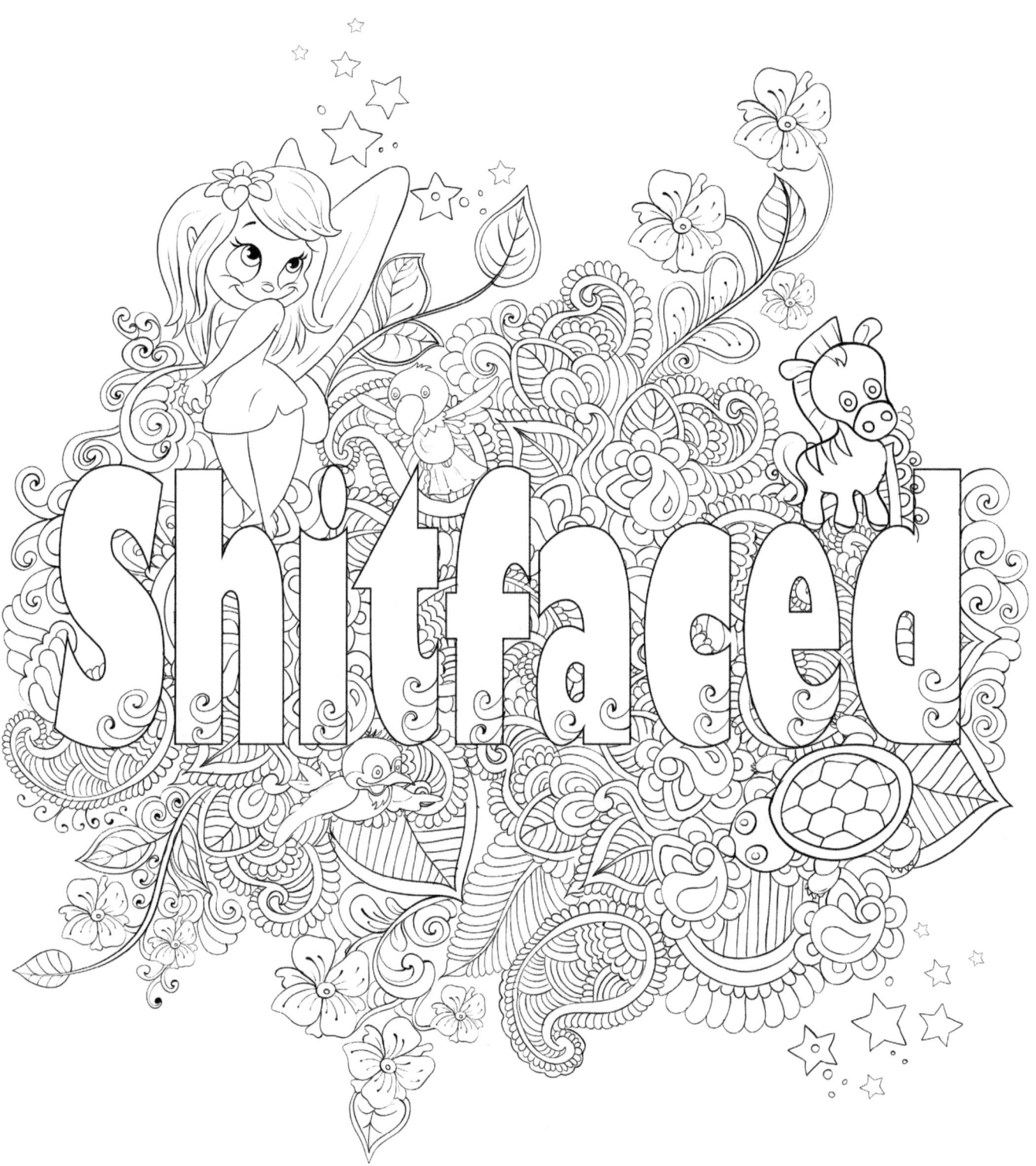

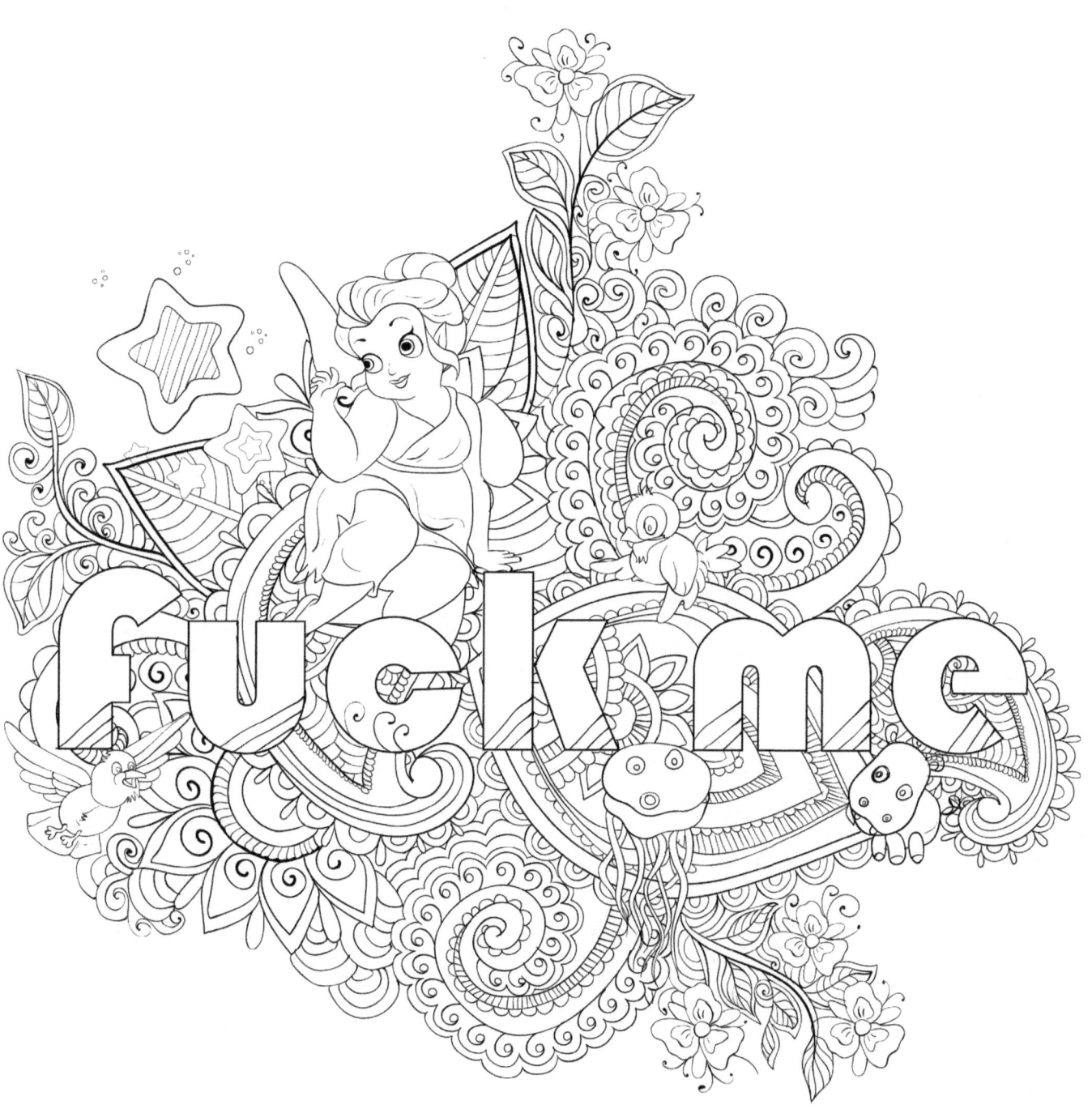

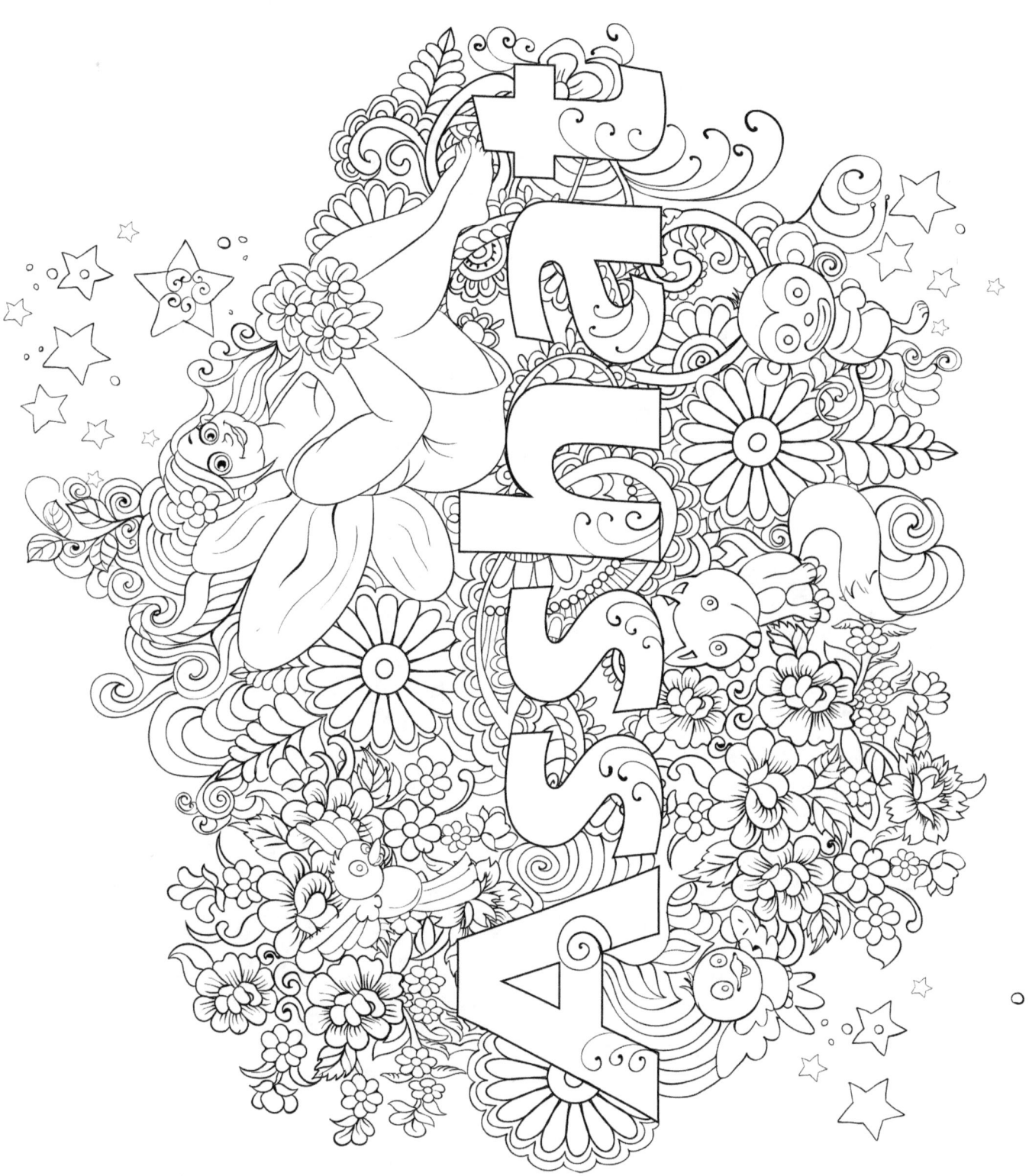

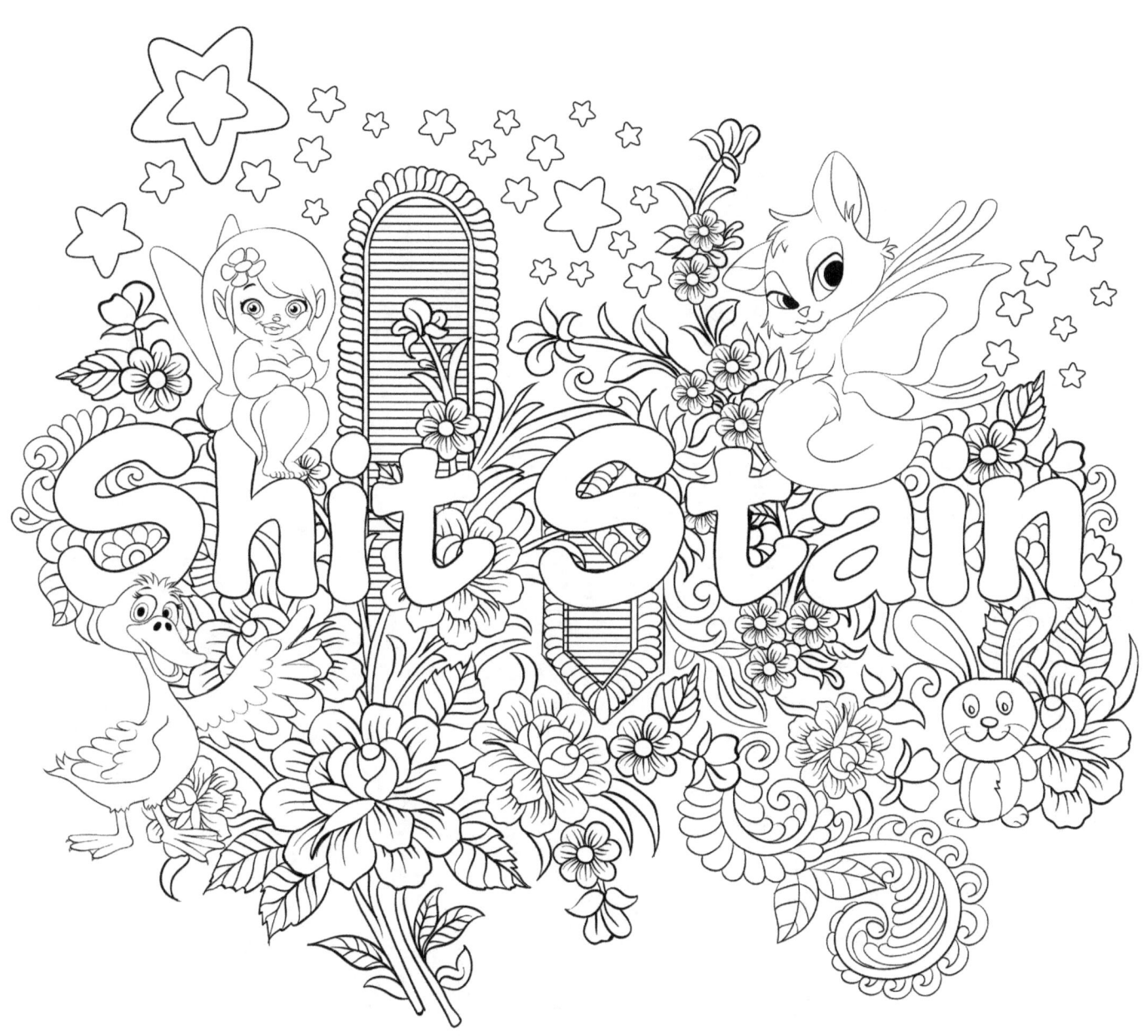

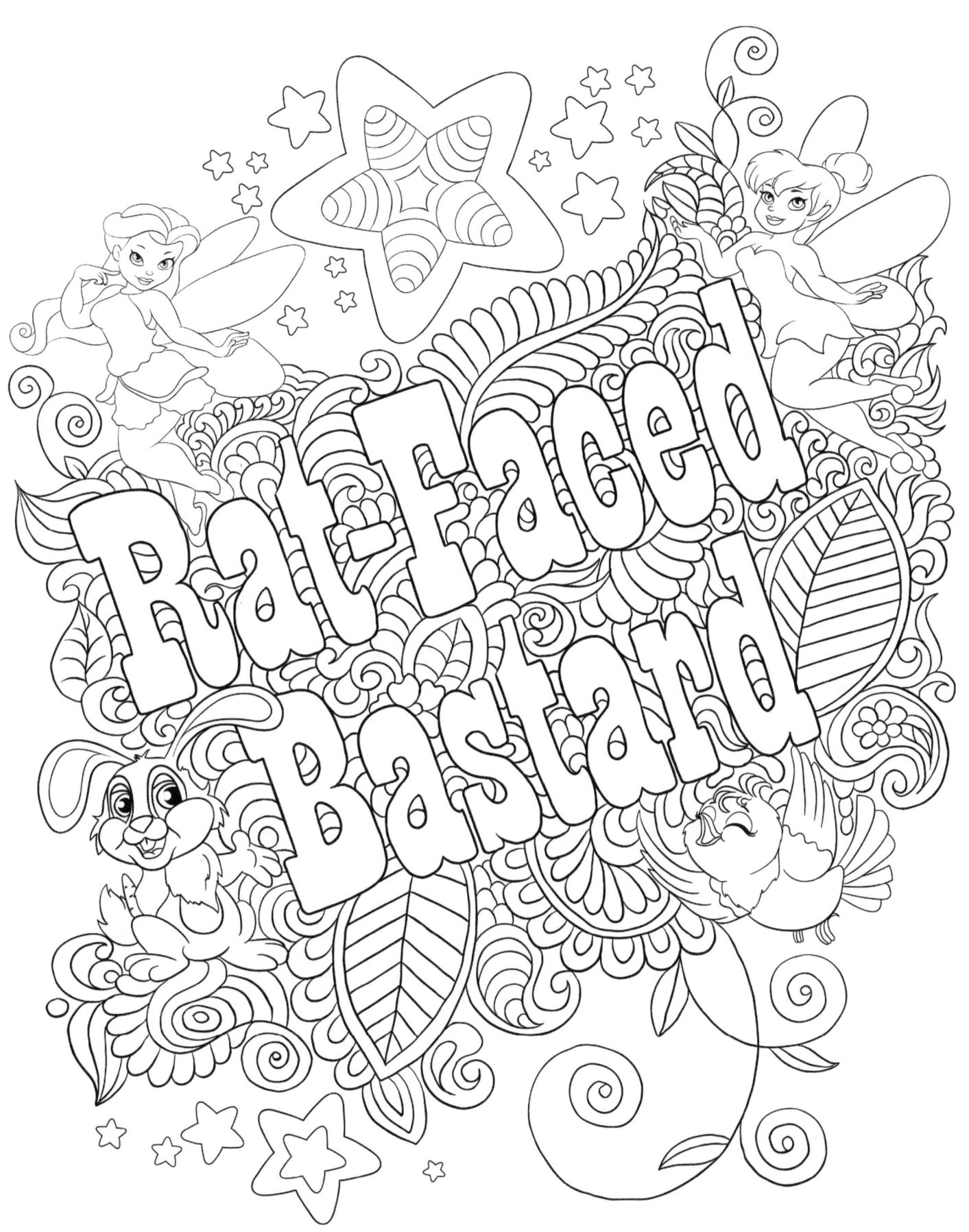

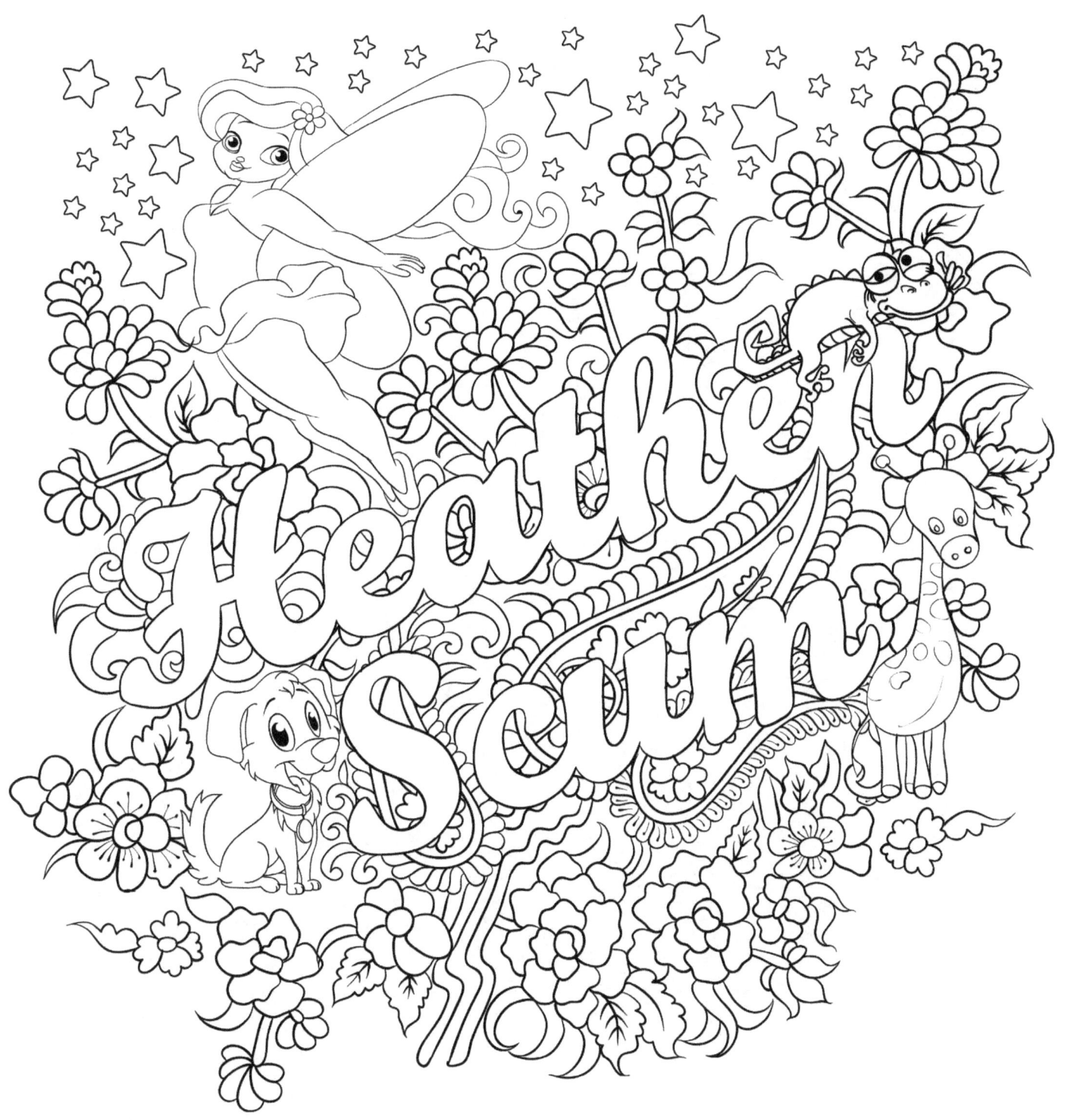

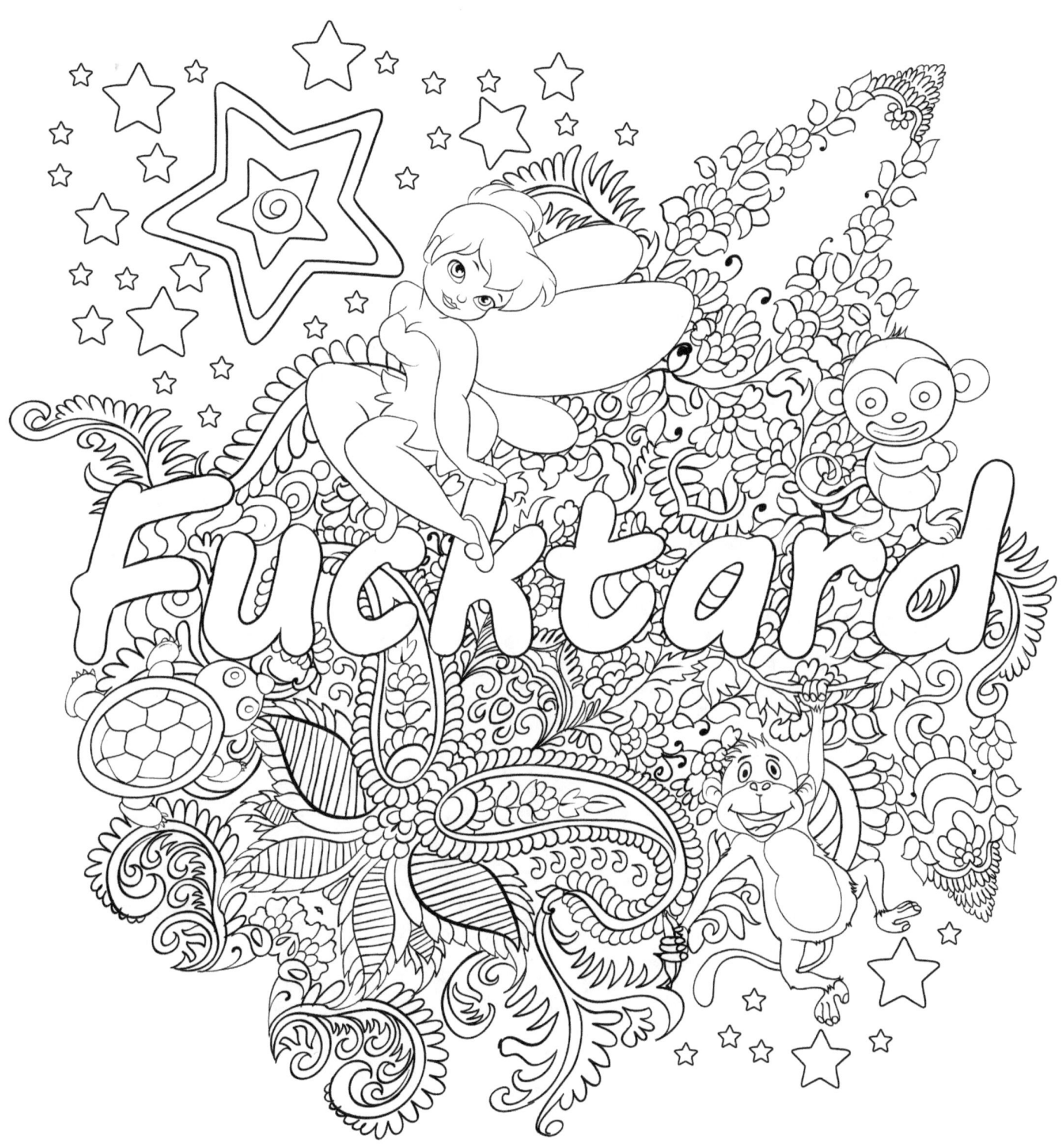

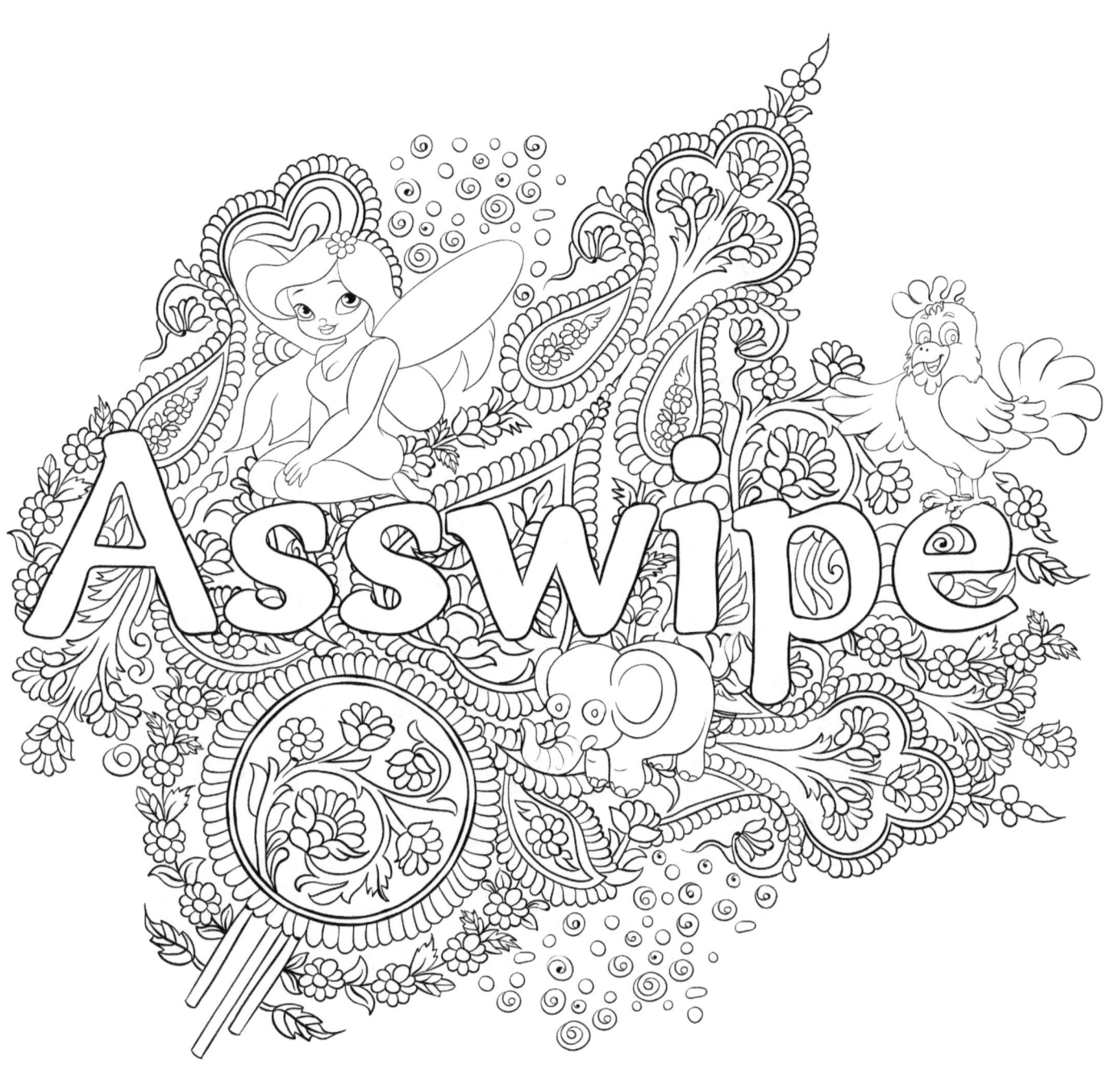

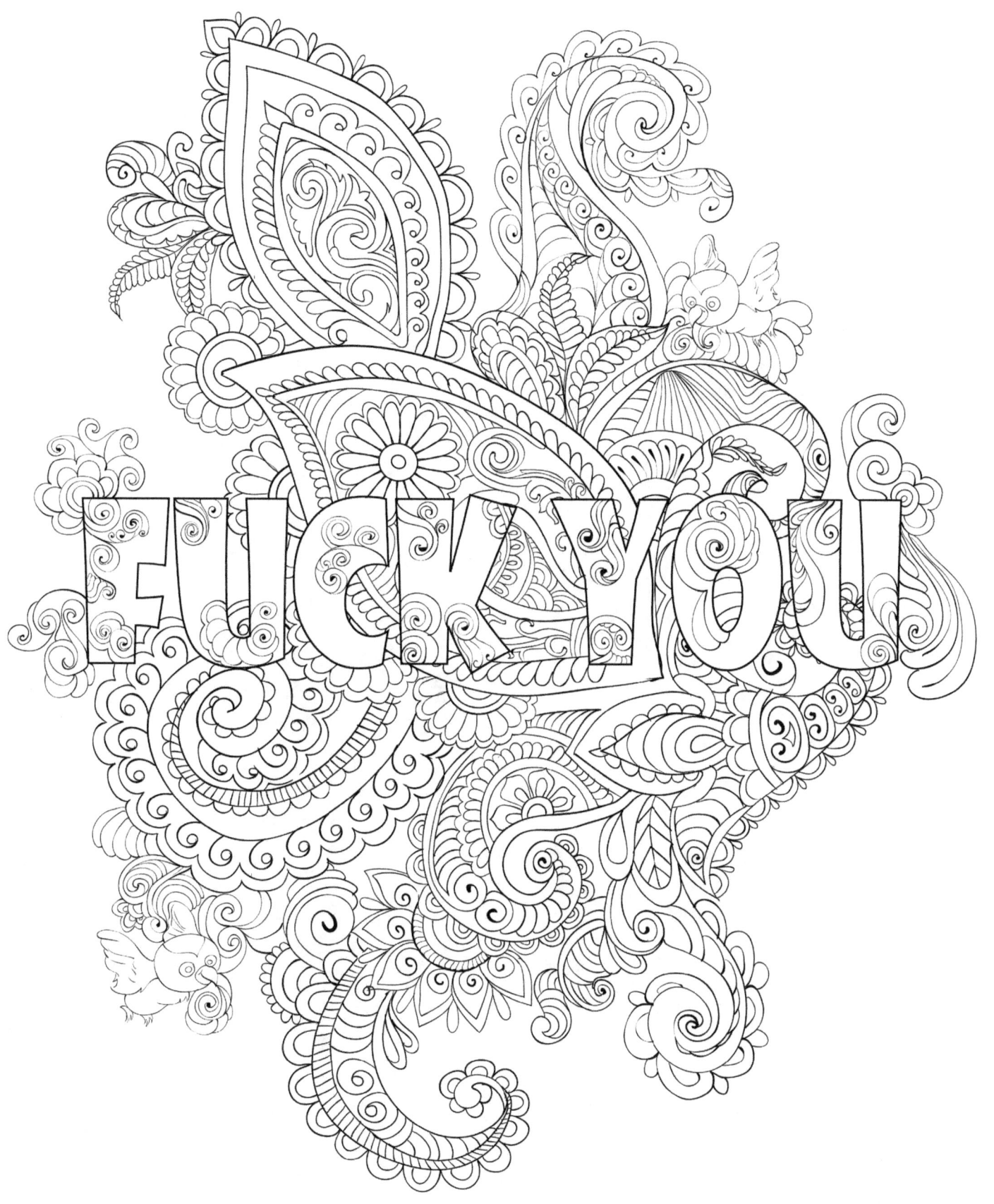

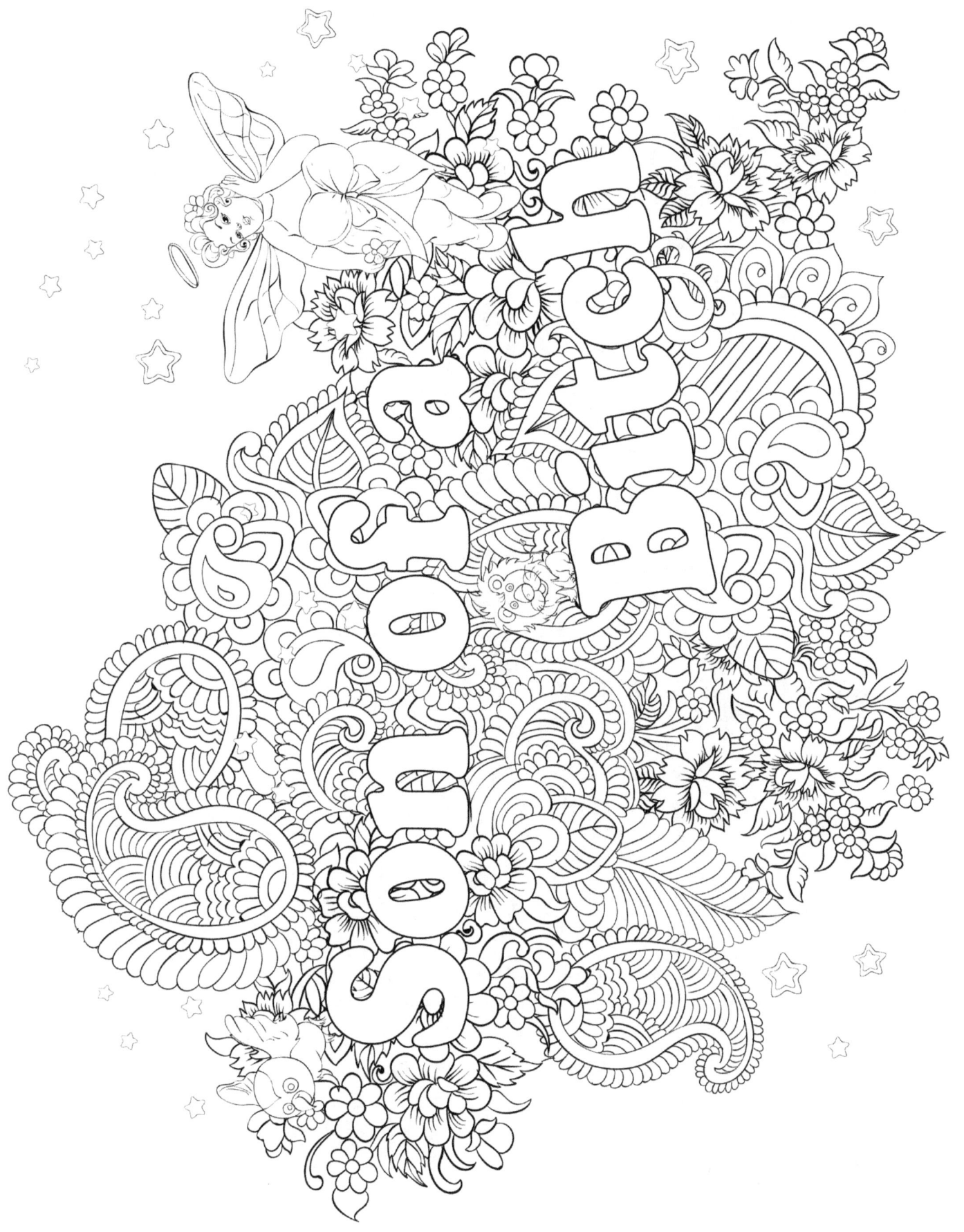

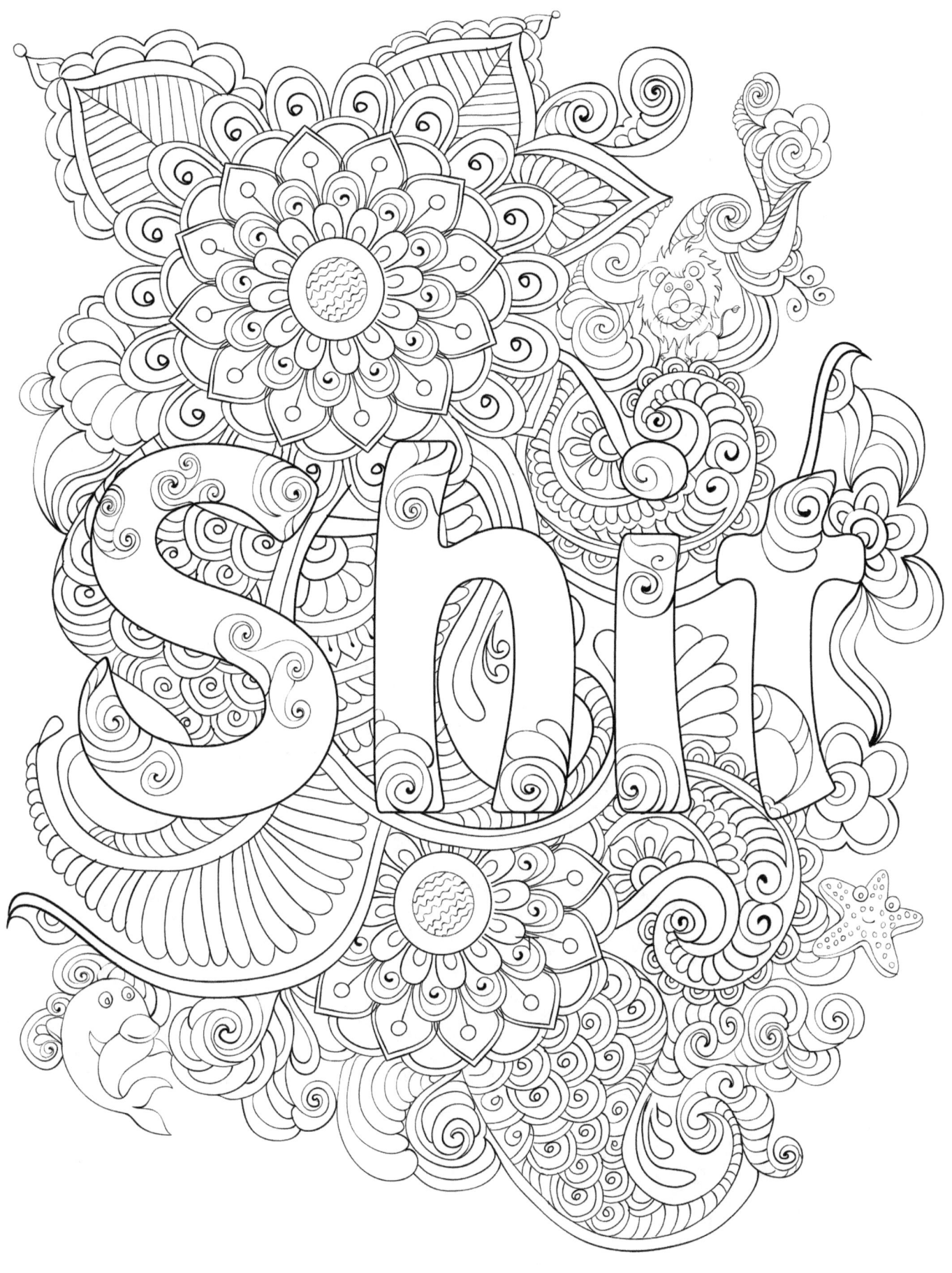

Free Bonus Book

$3.99 value electronic coloring book, easy to print out. Download your FREE book now:

http://CoolAdultColoringBooks.com

More: Check our website above for new books and special promotion deals…

www.ingramcontent.com/pod-product-compliance
Lightning Source LLC
Chambersburg PA
CBHW080636190526
45169CB00009B/3409